Deserts

To the One who created deserts.
—*Genesis* 1:9–10

Published by
PEACHTREE PUBLISHERS
1700 Chattahoochee Avenue
Atlanta, Georgia 30318-2112
www.peachtree-online.com

Text © 2007 by Cathryn P. Sill
Illustrations © 2007 by John C. Sill

Illustrations created in watercolor on archival quality 100% rag watercolor paper
Text and titles set in Novarese from Adobe Systems

Printed in Singapore
10 9 8 7 6 5 4 3 2 1
First Edition

Library of Congress Cataloging-in-Publication Data

Sill, Cathryn P., 1953-
  About habitats : deserts / written by Cathryn Sill ; illustrated by John Sill. -- 1st ed.
    p. cm.
  ISBN 978-1-56145-390-0
  1. Deserts--Juvenile literature. I. Sill, John, ill. II. Title.
  QH88 .S
  577.54--dc22
                        2006027699

Deserts

Written by **Cathryn Sill**   Illustrated by **John Sill**

PEACHTREE
ATLANTA

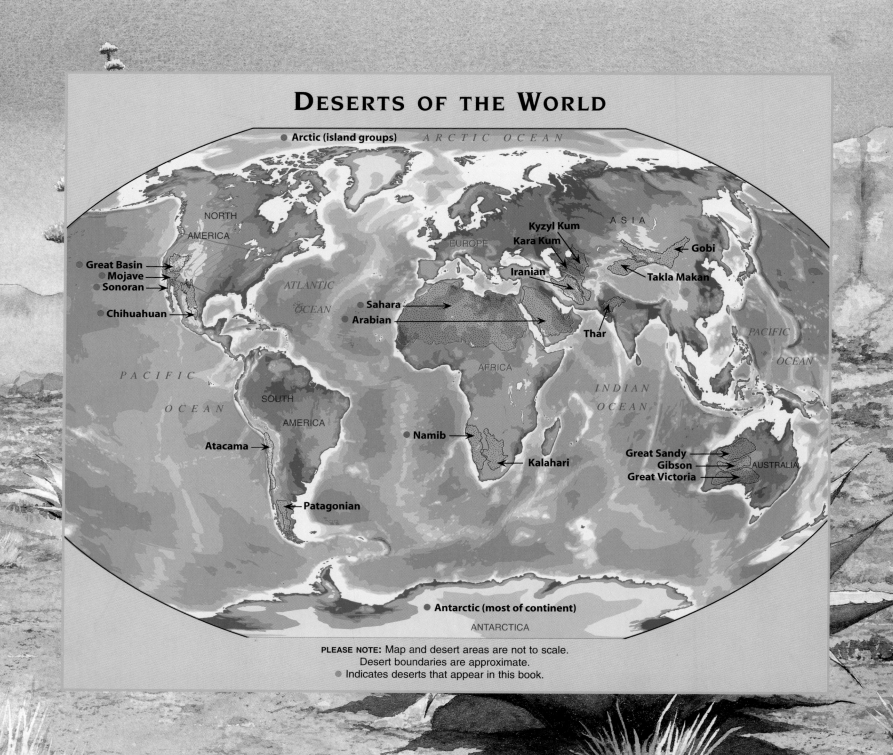

DESERTS OF THE WORLD

Arctic (island groups)

ARCTIC OCEAN

ASIA

Kyzyl Kum

Kara Kum

Gobi

NORTH
AMERICA

EUROPE

Great Basin

Mojave

Sonoran

Iranian

Takla Makan

ATLANTIC
OCEAN

Chihuahuan

Sahara

Arabian

Thar

AFRICA

PACIFIC
OCEAN

PACIFIC

SOUTH
AMERICA

INDIAN
OCEAN

OCEAN

Namib

Great Sandy

Atacama

Gibson

AUSTRALIA

Kalahari

Great Victoria

Patagonian

Antarctic (most of continent)

ANTARCTICA

PLEASE NOTE: Map and desert areas are not to scale.
Desert boundaries are approximate.
● Indicates deserts that appear in this book.

ABOUT HABITATS

Deserts

Deserts are dry places that get very little rain.

Some deserts are very hot.

Others can be very cold.

PLATE 3
GREAT BASIN DESERT

Common Raven
Big Sagebrush

Many deserts are covered with rocks.

PLATE 4
CHIHUAHUAN DESERT

Collared Lizard
Lechuguilla
Ocotillo

Some are sandy and covered with dunes.

Living things have special ways to survive in desert habitats. Some desert animals must go long distances to find water.

Others may burrow underground or find shade during the hottest part of the day.

Many desert animals hunt and eat only at night when temperatures are cooler.

Some desert animals wait until it rains to become active.

Plate 9
CHIHUAHUAN DESERT

Western Spadefoot Toad

Others get all the moisture they need from the food they eat.

The roots of desert plants have special ways
of gathering and storing water.

Some desert plants can store a lot of water in their stems.

Many desert plants are covered with wax that helps keep the water in their stems and leaves.

The seeds of some desert plants can stay in the ground for years, waiting until it rains enough for them to bloom and grow.

Some deserts do not get any rain. Their moisture comes from fog and dew.

PLATE 15
NAMIB DESERT

Fog-basking Beetle

An area in the desert that has water all of the time is called an oasis.

PLATE 16
SAHARA DESERT

Dromedary
Date Palm Tree

It is important to protect deserts and the animals and plants that live there.

PLATE 17
SONORAN DESERT

Organ Pipe Cactus
Curve-billed Thrasher
Costa's Hummingbird

DESERTS

Afterword

PLATE 1

A desert is an area that gets less than 10 inches of rainfall a year. The regions around the North and South Poles (Arctic and Antarctic), which are extremely cold and often covered in ice or snow, are considered deserts. Approximately one-fifth of the land on Earth is warm desert, and about one sixth is cold desert. Saguaro (*suh-wah-row*) cactuses grow in the Sonoran Desert, a warm desert in southern Arizona, California, and Mexico. They can live up to 200 years and grow to be 50 feet tall.

PLATE 2

In hot deserts, the daytime temperature can be over 120 degrees Fahrenheit. Because there are few clouds and very little moisture in the air to trap the heat from the sun, it can get cold at night. These cooler nighttime temperatures are important for the survival of desert life. Greater Roadrunners, which are common in the deserts of the Southwestern United States, pant to help keep their bodies cool when it is hot.

PLATE 3

Some deserts are cold for much of the year. During these cold times, precipitation comes in the form of snow. The plants and animals of North America's Great Basin Desert have to be able to survive freezing temperatures in winter as well as intense heat in summer. Plants such as Big Sagebrush and animals like Common Ravens are well adapted to the extremes in temperatures.

PLATE 4

Most deserts have sandy areas, but there are more rocky deserts than those completely covered by sand. The Chihuahuan Desert—known for its many mesas and mountains—is the largest in North America. Reptiles such as the Collared Lizard thrive in this hot climate; they are cold-blooded and their body temperatures adjust according to their surroundings.

PLATE 5

The Arabian Desert has the largest continuous area of sand in the world. The wind constantly moves the sand, causing changes in the size and shape of dunes. Arabian Oryx are desert antelope that became extinct in the wild because of over-hunting. Captive breeding programs have reintroduced the species into places where they used to live.

PLATE 6

Crowned Sandgrouse are able to live in the hottest, driest parts of the Sahara Desert in Africa. They may have to fly up to 30 miles to find water. The male sandgrouse wades in and lets the special feathers on his belly get soaking wet. Then he flies back to his nest and lets his babies drink from his wet feathers.

PLATE 7

Many animals find cooler temperatures and damper air just a few inches under the desert surface. Desert Tortoises burrow underground so that they can live in areas where the surface temperatures get above 140 degrees. Their burrows protect them from the heat in the summer and from the cold in the winter. Desert Cottontails find shelter under plants. If vegetation is scarce, they may take cover in the burrows of other animals.

PLATE 8

Fennecs are the smallest kind of wild dog. These desert foxes live in the Sahara and Arabian Deserts. Their thick fur is the same color as the sand and provides good camouflage. It also keeps them cool in hot weather and warm during cool nights when they hunt. They have fur on the soles of their feet, which makes it easier for them to run in the hot desert sand. Their huge ears help them find prey and avoid predators.

PLATE 9

Like other amphibians, Western Spadefoot Toads require a damp environment to keep their skin moist. They live in deep underground burrows, where they may spend eight to ten months during hot, dry weather. When the short rainy season begins, Western Spadefoot Toads come out to mate and lay their eggs. The eggs hatch in about two days, and the tadpoles quickly become adults so they can dig burrows before the rain puddles dry up.

PLATE 10

Desert Kangaroo Rats live in the driest areas of North America. They can live without ever having to drink water. Kangaroo rats come out at night when the air is cooler and moister to feed on seeds, plants, and insects. They use their fur-lined cheek pouches to carry and store food.

PLATE 11

The Dahlia Cactus (left) has a large swollen root for storing water and food. The roots of the Dahlia Cactus are much larger than the stems. Other plants like the Creosote Bush (right) grow many roots to collect every bit of the water in the ground around it. The Creosote Bush is found in all of the hot deserts of North America.

PLATE 12

The insides of cactus stems are made of spongy tissue that is able to store water. The thick stems of barrel cactuses have ridges that allow them to expand as water is soaked up (left). As the water is used, the stem shrinks (right). Cactuses have spines instead of leaves. Fishhook Barrel Cactuses get their name from their long hooked spines.

PLATE 13

Many desert plants have waxy surfaces that protect them from the sun and help keep water inside. The Big Bend Century Plant gets its name from the mistaken belief that it only blooms every hundred years. A century plant can actually bloom after 20 or 30 years. The bloom stalks are 10 to 20 feet tall, and the blossoms provide food for birds, insects, and bats.

PLATE 14

The seeds of some desert plants can stay in the dry soil for years waiting for just the right conditions before they become active. Once the rain comes and the seeds germinate, these desert wildflowers grow, bloom, and make seeds quickly before the land dries out again. Desert wildflowers provide nectar for bees, butterflies, and other insects, as well as food for larger animals. Smaller animals such as rodents eat some of the seeds.

PLATE 15

When temperatures drop at night, dew forms. This is an important source of water for desert plants and animals. Coastal deserts such as the Namib Desert in Africa get moisture from fog blowing in from the ocean. Fog-basking Beetles are able to drink water provided by this fog. They stand with their heads down and let the fog collect on their bodies. The drops of water roll down their backs into their mouths.

PLATE 16

The water in a desert oasis usually comes from an underground spring or pool. More plants are able to grow at oases since water is always available. Some oases are large enough to support many people and have cities built around them. Others are very small and may provide water for just a few plants and animals. Dromedaries are well adapted to life in the desert. They can drink up to 13 gallons of water at a time, then go for several days without another drink. Dromedaries store fat in the humps on their backs for times when food is scarce.

PLATE 17

Desert environments are very fragile because of their harsh conditions. They support remarkable plants and animals that cannot live anywhere else on Earth. Many human activities—including development, mining, farming, ranching, and even tourism—are endangering deserts. We need to be careful to protect all natural environments so the wide variety of plants and animals can live and work together to keep our planet safe and healthy.

GLOSSARY

BIOME—an area such as a desert or tropical rain forest that shares the same types of plants and animals

ECOSYSTEM—a community of living things and their environment

HABITAT—the place where animals and plants live (A desert can support many types of habitats—from nests in a cactus plant to underground burrows, from sandy soil to a rocky surface.)

Burrow—to make a hole in the ground (Some animals live in holes made by other animals.)

Cactus—a plant of dry regions, usually with spines instead of leaves and fleshy tissue for holding moisture

Damp—slightly wet

Dew—small drops of water that form from moisture in the air when temperatures get cooler at night

Dune—a hill of sand piled up and shaped by the wind

Extinct—no longer living

Fog—tiny drops of water in the air close to the ground

Germinate—to start to grow from a seed

Moisture—slight wetness

Precipitation—rain, snow, or hail

Survive—to stay alive

BIBLIOGRAPHY

BOOKS

LIFE IN THE DESERTS by Lucy Baker (Scholastic)

DK NATURE ENCYCLOPEDIA (Dorling Kindersley Children)

EYEWITNESS BOOKS: DESERT by Miranda MacQuitty (Dorling Kindersley Children)

DESERT PLANTS by Susan Reading (Facts on File)

ANIMALS BY HABITAT: ANIMALS OF THE DESERT by Stephen Savage (Raintree)

THE YOUNG OXFORD BOOK OF ECOLOGY by Michael Scott (Oxford University Press).

AMERICA'S DESERTS: GUIDE TO PLANTS AND ANIMALS by Marianne D. Wallace (Fulcrum Publishing)

WEBSITES

www.mbgnet.net/

www.desertusa.com/life.html

www.desertmuseum.org

www.inchinapinch.com/hab_pgs/terres/desert/desert.htm

Also by the Sills:
The ABOUT... series

ABOUT THE SILLS

Cathryn Sill, a former elementary school teacher, is the author of the acclaimed ABOUT… series. With her husband John and her brother-in-law Ben Sill, she coauthored the popular bird-guide parodies, A FIELD GUIDE TO LITTLE-KNOWN AND SELDOM-SEEN BIRDS OF NORTH AMERICA, ANOTHER FIELD GUIDE TO LITTLE-KNOWN AND SELDOM-SEEN BIRDS OF NORTH AMERICA, and BEYOND BIRDWATCHING, all from Peachtree Publishers.

John Sill is a prize-winning and widely published wildlife artist who illustrated the ABOUT… series and coauthored the FIELD GUIDES and BEYOND BIRDWATCHING. A native of North Carolina, he holds a B.S. in Wildlife Biology from North Carolina State University.

The Sills live and work in Franklin, North Carolina.

Fred Eldredge, Creative Image Photography

Books in the ABOUT… series

ISBN 1-56145-028-6 HC
ISBN 1-56145-147-9 PB

ISBN 1-56145-141-X HC
ISBN 1-56145-174-6 PB

ISBN 1-56145-183-5 HC
ISBN 1-56145-233-5 PB

ISBN 1-56145-207-6 HC
ISBN 1-56145-232-7 PB

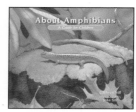

ISBN 1-56145-234-3 HC
ISBN 1-56145-312-9 PB

ISBN 1-56145-256-4 HC
ISBN 1-56145-335-8 PB

ISBN 1-56145-038-3 HC
ISBN 1-56145-364-1 PB

ISBN 1-56145-301-3 HC
ISBN 1-56145-405-2 PB

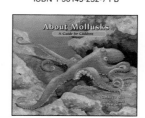

ISBN 1-56145-331-5 HC

ISBN 1-56145-358-7 HC